GW00708370

The Dedalus Press

editor John F Deane

EASTER SNOW

GERARD FANNING

DUBLIN 1992

The Dedalus Press
24 The Heath
Cypress Downs
Dublin 6W

Cover design by Paul Barrass

Acknowledgements:

Austin Clarke Broadsheet, Cyphers, Connacht Tribune
(Writing in the West), The Irish Times, The Irish Press
(New Irish Writing), Krino, Paris Atlantic, Poetry Ireland
Review,Rhinosceros, The Simon Anthology, Soundings 2,
St Stephens, UCD Broadsheet, RTE (The Poet's Choice,
Appraisal).

The Dedalus Press receives financial assistance from
An Chomhairle Ealaíon, The Arts Council, Ireland

for my mother
and for Barney Fanning (d. 25/11/81)

CONTENTS

1 *The Conquest of Djouce*

2 *Unregistered Papers*

1. The Conquest of Djouce

WAITING ON LEMASS

It is nineteen sixty two
Or three, and we are playing soccer
In fields laced with the sheen of bamboo.

In the air that turns
Amber as sally rods,
Somewhere out of picture,

A man is hitting golf balls
As if there were no tomorrow.
He slouches towards the sycamore shade

Searching for what couples
Might be lying in the seed beds
Or that tall grass

Loosely flecked with rye.
None the wiser, we walk home
Under the beige satellites

That roll in the ether of themselves,
While all about,
A blaze of radio perfume

Speaks of a man
Moving his ships on soup-like waters,
Or a president slumped

On his girlfriend's knee,
As here our long druid leaders
Wander through the closing zones,

Their autistic god
Commanding options in the street,
The curfew till the white hour.

AUGUST IN WILLIAMSTOWN

I watch the white moon rising,
A tantalising spark of God's benign face
Revelling in our bewildered eyes.

As I walk, owls croon,
And a wide grin of scent cruises
In the lawn's lavish spaces.

Moving down through Wicklow's
Stretching estates, slipping into
The mask of ease, I grasp

A tended landscape, bordered gardens –
Elements I can understand.
Even Calary, desolate and ice-clear

In the dwindling autumn light
Welcomes me. I am at home.
See this smile –

It perfects my dual life,
A sinner erasing sin
I spend six months in the odour

Of prayer, while my face shrinks
From this chalice. If, occasionally
I head for the city, I slide

Like the moon through thin branches
Down the too crowded streets.
There I recall cold flagstones

A perpetual murmuring, and stare
At living gods, their smiles
Resigned to a surfeit.

PHILBY'S APOSTLES ON MERRION STRAND

All of these beaches –
mist drenched in wide lagoons
were drawn out neatly for cartographers.

Why then do men come
hauling seismometers, their tripods
straining for the lateral view?

Silently they position
to observe the wingbeat migrations
of a city's carriages.

They may as well define
the waves gasping breath
as they check for new terminals,

for here they have come
to the outer limits,
tracing the flaw in the rounded eye,

the fault in the world's Chippendale.
Watch them tune their cackling radios
of bird-song and wind-song

staring eastward as though
a life's objective could ring less clear
down the crowded airwaves.

Meanwhile a world of talking heads
pass by their doors; quiet manoeuvres
belie hidden purpose.

NOTES ON HOME

1. *In the City*

The city stays awake all night
sparked in occasional carlight
and we lie down, together or alone
as all the metals groan
or purr to a dead stop.

In single rooms, phones idling
we dream out across
rooftops, empty warehouses
where lost consignments
still flash aimlessly
on a raised map of the world.

Through the workings
of a city's widening parishes
cruising taxis waltz,
eyes diminishing in a dawn rise
of radios and banging screens.

And we rise
waking in the bright shuffle
of paperthin messages
brought down the icy roads
to these, our halls
and silent window boxes.

2. *The Lawn*

Hoe the black clay till its spur
Resembles the dust of the moon map,
Let all the sandy seas mirror the pantry floor
And let the calm that follows down
Play through the agonies
Of the fickle pollen storms.
Might everything find its level –
Field-cow wheat, dandelion and thistle,
The grain and the tassel of a sage trampoline.
Now as shooting stars descend
I correct small contour flaws,
Pencil stroke a declining magic
On staves for the next rendition,
And dream of a pine needle perfection
Where your hint might be the blueish vein,
The charcoal in the bush soul,
The resin nibbling the membrane.

3. *An Evening in Booterstown*

After cold days taking photographs
confirming the nearest coastline
I look from your window
and imagine how the tramp fields
might have turned to a wax impression
of the sea's other shores. Turning
like a folded mirror, or growing
in detail just as these blank papers
on the tray near the alcove
swim through their blue chemicals
and gather the last of Dublin's
refracted light. See there
emerging from the covering darkness
of lintels, bay-windows and shut
doors, a circle of light corrects
the skyline. Like any brief town
time has polished it, with
the sea-marsh and the harbour wall
to a pale permanence.

4. *The Belfast Train*

Though we don't set our watches anymore
we note the temporary withdrawals
and file the small faults
in a flawless system. Round Dundalk

tracks may remain empty for days –
the ghostly carriages wintering
in the blank fields. Word gets through,
buses awkwardly skirt the pocket miles.

If we sit till we comprehend
like gangers repairing the timetables,
we may think the random suicides
are powdered with pockmarks

and tossed beneath the train
as an afterthought. Or, if lives
in the stilt-house junction boxes
tick out their last

in a whispering discontent,
the automatic levers are watched
yet working on
whistling through the late departures.

5. *Within a Mile of Dublin*

Waiting for the new ice age
A fifties rucksack slung in the hall
Panniers fading into survival,
And here a bureau filled with maps –
All the bright cities that spiral out
From the paving stones of parishes
To the glass of the world savannah.

See how my child-like drawings
Foretold the smoky photographs
That swam through faded oxygen,
And see how I pretend to know
The swirl of the earth's weather,
The politics of dwindling satellites –
Trying to imagine the lost caresses
Meandering in space. So if I draw
Boundaries ravenous for acreage
I still remember where the coffee-
Stained villages are breathing
Beneath the listless reservoirs.

OCCUPATIONS

Germans over Belfast, 1941

From the high sun of Germany
we climb into the dark,
a steel pack of light diviners.

Below, our giant homeland
cautiously gathers the seas,
trains the sun and smiles up

at our glinting journeys. Perhaps
her wise stare will chart
the blank no-man's land

which rides down on us
from the cold north; for clearly
the world is a closing fist.

Europe's hinge tightening
as we veer north from Dublin.

Outside, the constant radar unfurls
like a red spool of brain –
picks out pocketed holdings,

mild couplings and lights
crawling up the narrow roads.

This sleepy tackle of stars
is their Maginot Line,
a honeycomb of drowned valleys

eating through the land
like a changeling crop
yielding to its own seasons.

In the confused fires we build
a tatter of signals:
our life's definition now,

a tired odyssey in a world
grown warm with our cold grip.

ALMA REVISITED

No trace of the north marsh polder,
The hooker sloops off Rush,
The girl reading under the verandah.

I could lay Saint-Exupéry aside,
And search like his swab biplane
For that polyester strip.

But I wake, and the loop round the bawn
Shows the hotel not yet extended.
In *Árd Na Mara, Lisheen Villa,*

A mild bel canto voice
Fills the tented air with soothing sleep,
While you stand on Ford-strewn beaches,

In a bitter quail light,
Characters from a dust bowl depression,
Smiling despite the terror of the future.

MAKING DEALS

Landscape painters, photographers,
have us standing awkwardly
ignoring the image maker –
it's only half a lie,

for we are the ciphers
that give you what you see.

All round the growing cold streets
men are making deals.
They meet in bars, hush,
bend heads and gesture

in the underhand.
Within their splayed fingers
the cluttered microfilm exchange
of blueprints passed

all in the ease
of casual conversation.

Where we made the streets
gaps became alleyways
and men rode out in cars
to marshal the intelligence

of addresses. Now as money
abandons the derelict sites
they circle on stilts
attempting to cohere the subterfuge.

Watch as the centre slowly hollows
and cables map the countryside.

THE VIEW FROM ERRISBEG

Robert Lloyd Praeger
Called it the best in Ireland.
Climbing with three children

Where ice or bulldozed shale
Must have wrestled with shape,
I saw the thunder of the north west passage

Pouring into a pagan bowl,
And through a muslin sheen of horseflies
I gazed like Praeger

At the magnificent loneliness of the lakes.
Weeks later in a cowering Dublin,
I stand in a blue light

And watch the smoky figures
Begin to emerge,
My long lost Franklin

Whose loneliness charged the incidental
Into a world-weary search
For a safe passage

Out of God's bleak stare.
I stack the inky photographs
(Engraved miniature journeys)

And sense wild indigo
Peppering my skin,
Prompting a medical note

Or a bruised tattoo
To rise from the cracked calamine
For all the lost galleons

Moaning on their beds of brine.
Perhaps a leisured life
Becomes its own fabric,

As here in braided light,
Placenames fade with the ochre sun,
My folded map tucks like an alpenstock

And I drift into the lull of mid-evening,
Dreaming of an astronaut
Who descends through hoar frost,

His visor blank with detail,
All the thin bleached drawings
Of our winter trading ships

Locked in the purple ice;
And already in the *National Geographic*
The mock-up is conceived.

CLIFDEN STATION

I ride the necklace of roads
on this island
but never reach the sea.
All around me hollow stretches
topple into the evening sun
and the sky begins
to fall again with frost.

I try, as I can, to understand
these wintry acres –
a soldier's nightmare of no cover,
looted trucks cradling the ditches as
mild corrosions burn the moon-white fields.

Above me, the whining transit planes
circle like the night's static –
a million voices on my radio.
I skirt the perimeters of stations,
the yellow main streets,
searching for some treeless rendezvous
where messages transfer.

WITH SIOBHÁN

We walk sluicing these rainfields
talking of other people
never ourselves, as if
growing side by side in the actual
were all that was.

Yet see there
like a lunar diagram
or there
like a breast behind calico –
the lines of other lives.

In these bald fields
chambered graves
reveal like an x-ray's grey definition
God's face staring back –
a shadow on the Andes slopes.

Here is a litter trove of ingenuity
layered like floor panelling
beneath the ground.
Overnight abandoned mines
clink and gleam

endless highways
buckling in a rich seam.
And where I have left you
walking on alone
I see the waggon trails

where they hauled
the teepee stones,
a village of homage
to a god
as bright as our own.

PHILBY IN IRELAND

Nightfall, and we have driven out
From the warm lights. The thick fog
Circling the hill's base, corrodes
Our white car as it stalks the incline.

From this high air we can see
The crawling streets, trucks and buses
Wheeling in their correct motions –
Trails leaving a decipher of rests.

Somewhere in this parallel of workings
Men catalogue the labyrinth of the city
And deep in its crushed underbelly
We meet and copy the blueprints

Of a world drawn out on long papers,
Lives collapse if we fail, for our work
Though underhand, is significant,
Like priests we are diligent or we do not

Believe. Abandoning cars, we move down
To the murmuring inlets, wide lagoons
Cheeping at the breaker wall. We sail out
Adrift in the wider perspective.

THE ROAD TO THE SKELLIGS

We have outstayed our welcome.
Taking only what we can carry
We walk south, a geiger sense
Of food and survival building

In our prayers a brief taste
Of God's companionship. He sends all.
Yet daily see how our sacrifices refine
To the practical. These planned escapes

Are far removed from the passive
Latin incantations that struggle
In a previous intelligence.
As if to deny us now the ocean

Rises, while the rain's waltzing feet
Tripples islands in the image
Of our amazed stores of gold
Melting to a powder of foam.

Slowly the road is giving in.
Even here it steeplejacks to the rim
Of a saucer bog and falls
Down into the Glen's mouth

Where the Skelligs flicker –
A monstrance jagged with rare stone.
We will sail the drowned valley
In prayer, safe from God and man.

GARRETT BARRY VISITS INIS OIRR

My eyes sink to the ticking clock
of a thumping currach
straddling the sea; muffled conversations

surround me in this cloudy bowl.
Sitting on a low stool
in the sunlit doorway,

crayon light halves the room,
turf smoke, pipe smoke,
cradling the drawn faces

appearing before me. As I play
my eyes shut like a silent hall
cool and envious of the sun,

while my father's music
builds in harmonies
colliding in my memory.

I hone timbres of foot tappings,
the fussy sounds of dancers feet
like a tuning orchestra,

release the stopped air
of this compact church organ
resting on my knee. Glossed round

the old men at the hedgerows
I see the map of future tunes,
and further through the shawled fields –

the incomprehensible beauties
of the lake roads; mountain silence
a perfect sound, I perfect it.

THE FINAL MANOEUVRE

Living the middle life
Caught between lovers
I was prepared for the holocaust

That never came.
Crossing years like days
On a schoolboy's calendar

Tracking without retreat
I was the inexorable traveller
Pursuing my wounded grail.

On that chill November evening
In Glenmalure, I could have owned
The whole of Wicklow

But fences would have encouraged thieves.
So, turning now in this cocoon
of soft noises

I stare smiling
Toward the spark of the living,
Their coloured flags weaving

A cosy fever, their loves
Chased by clock-hands
And a life's debris.

Lying in this damp chair
A festering in the moor-swamp's side
I draw a pulled curtain of hair

To keep the seasons in ebb-tide;
While this axle of earth
Conceals me, composes my relief.

LARGO

They found a body in the uplands,
A village sleeper, curled in the furred snow
Not caring to go on.

When we examine the ice clean repose
A chill seeps through the jerkin sleeve,
The wire glasses telescope a score of winters,

And the padding of a strip of pine
Becomes the blip in the earlobe
Attaching to his heartspace.

Might we also carry our saline bag
Over the loughs and tarot,
A journey through the fleecy undertow,

Past the crossroads post office,
Where pension money and stamps
Watermark to a like regret?

Or perhaps, if we peered into the hard lime
That freezes the channels in the trees,
We too could stare back admiring it all –

The world events comically coming apart,
And love, the measure of our lives,
Billeted one month for every year.

GEOGRAPHERS

1.

Dragon-flies dart
in the earth's smoke
as we race up country.
The road is a crucifix

of turns, wind
a dull chant
pulling us to the Boyne
and beyond.

When we reach
the white-washed
courtyards of Meath,
its silent tumuli are

drifting and the mist
sprawls a white coverlet
screening their bright dance.
In dense, loud bars

we sense the waves'
pocketed beatings,
and careering in
the moon's soft tug

we toss the harsh music.
Outside, in the cold glow
of the world, frost
crafts glass and cobbles

to topography, and further
through a running contour
of mounds and clay crosses
a cluster of larks

sing dreary lullabies
to their unborn. It reaches us
as faint voices
maddening comprehension.

2.

Perhaps the drizzle
will subside
and we will map
that village of grass;

meantime like monks
we make jealous copy
of their neat
choir's discipline,

build an inventory
of the composer's silence –
for as quiet musicians
our wasted lives are spent

farming a stolen pasture,
giving orders
in a lost tongue.
In our haste

we have left this village
behind and the path
through the fields
locks to a gold brooch

of indecision,
pinning to the ground's
bruised skin its curled
loam. We must begin

again, trust only
the earth's booming,
straining to detail
its mechanism.

If, suckling on the mind's
music, we grow a tougher mime,
then we can sharpen
the tongue's reed,

imagine a space –
the wild dens
we dream about,
contented silence.

THE CONQUEST OF DJOUCE

Even on the simplest journey
Doubts may cloud the familiar.
Consider the walk from Djouce

Down to the barnyard of the world;
Hauling sextants, compasses
And a dull stevedore calm,

We can't conceive of lost cargoes,
Or how pot-bellied planes
Could fail and slowly condense

In a swelter of rambling vine.
Yet miles from radio signals,
The morse that brings up the day,

Land dreams of the human gaze.
For there is only a view, a scattering of tan,
Broken fences rusting into local colour

And for twenty miles around,
Pluming fires in the cinnamon sky.
Where Powerscourt mulls in distant heat,

Burton or Speke might rise to stare
From their floating canopy of malaria.
They could imagine The Nile

Meandering down the page to its legend.
But Djouce is just what it seems –
A downy floor transmitting to elsewhere

The arc of our particular North Star,
And the boundaries are occasional,
Like the fleece that translates appearances

Into the cumulus of the view.
The evening coming slowly in,
Trails our bivouac through the ozone,

And the figure waving like a metronome,
Is *the Eskimo in his skin canoe,*
The only one who ever came through.

INTERIM MEMO TO GETTY

I should write about the long walk
Down from Mount Brown,

The pension visit, living alone enquiries,
Dust streets and tenements,

The handhold and foothold
Where Magritte might confuse

A windowsill with a chimney breast,
Or watch the floral wallpaper surround

Xeroxed across the sky.
But I sit all day in your open-plan,

Watching men point from a building site,
Fill their geometry in tin-smith coloumns

So the rising scaffold of corridors
Can store the heat of the sun.

Perhaps the frost that gathers round us all
Confuses the act with its document,

As the sliding past, the fabulous seepage,
Drains from private meter rooms

And our world sways in the air
On arms of glass intrigue.

MAYDAY ON GRIFFITH AVENUE

The Irish Sea sweats like a benign lake
In this midnight heat, two miles off.
Where asphalt merges with steel
And car-fins part the rain trees,
I dream of the ocean's rising,
How small effects like some insect genocide
Has the sea mildly pouring here,
Over lawns, railed basements;
And while the edgy foam and spirit level
Shunts in the city's sidings,
All the scattered families watch
The swaying sun in their elsewhere,
The threat in the wounded stratosphere.

GAS

A man is taking readings
Of pump and pressure
As the red fanlight,
That bloom in the western sky
Comes down from all around.

The last cars circle the globe
As he checks the oilcans,
The switch on *Mobilgas,*
And settles in the lee alcove
Where his soft-back thriller
Waits in its glove of chrome.

If he bothers to lock the outhouse
He will see how someone has scrawled
A message on the washroom mirror.

EAST OF THE PECOS

I live in the city manager's
inherited dream,
far from the badlands
sagebrush and sombrero

of the sierra foothills,
rather the cap and lavender face
towelled to a neat complexion.
Out from the plywood shavings

all the new line houses
spreadeagle and recline,
a treeless prairie
in its first winter:

children stopping screaming
joggers setting out
or coming into land
and overhead the teatime flight

from Heathrow, bored executives
looking down on us.
Each night, road lights
trigger with the dark

family cars homing exhausted
to their thin white shrouds,
while Howth Head scrambles
the excited signals

from the North,
and lapsing in our private dreams
we covet the blue imaginings,
the spark and metal

out over the Irish Sea.
As world events
break more violently,
I check the bus journeys,

the train's halt,
the road that slowly fills with cars
and marvel at natural manoeuvres undisturbed.
Each morning we wait

and all the minor details
of our future are retold
as though the world could possibly know
its own course

depending on us merely
to ride out in the choreography
of lightning touches,
while contracting streets

blunder like moths to the greens,
a trail boss eye, fixed
for the railway, the jug of commerce
and the saddle-weary horizon.

ORIENTEERING WITH ELIZABETH

Here is the report of a man
Walking out to the white valleys,
Breathing the mind-expanding air

Of that blind corrie
Which might hide the North Pole,
And carrying nothing

But the webbed gauze of himself.
I would give him
A radio filled with static,

A glowing stencil of food stations
And some whispered ingenuity
To fend the air of the laconic tundra.

But why leave the land of the living
When echoes of shouts
Career in the deadened lines of snow,

And ice in that sheer aquamarine
Swims down to the hot seas?
I am thinking now of how

You came to me one Christmas –
I showed you words
About love in the tropics

And you tensed as I reached
For the quiet sun of your breast,
Wandering in the visionlines

I weakened to impress.
In the almost certainty of future,
Through half sightings

You secrete the microfilm of all love
As though you knew all about
The mythical North Pole

And how it should stand
Like a painting of itself
Drifting in a circle of elms.

DAYTRIP TO VANCOUVER ISLAND

1.

We drove through the spine of the island –
Occasional clay crosses, where pockets of lives
Wait for rain and the mailman.

Reclining on the invisible grain of the world,
Their lock-up doors, endless gardens,
Dandle like uncharted nerve ends

And screen the uncut land, which must lie
Where the roads are still being planned.
In a weigh station, burning *Mobilgas*

I bought a card of Mount St. Helens
Hoping to send it to you,
A slight tremor to conceal

Like the shy scooped up lunar dust
Or the ash that basks here about
In a relaxed stare, on temperance houses

Salvation army platforms
And the batten wooden concaves
Of the various sun worshippers.

2.

The sea at Victoria was no surprise –
Couples promenading, gazing at Japan,
Horizons defined in snug harbour lights

All mapped, all comprehended
Like the fading zones of space.
Nightfall, and we rode the ferry-ride

Back to our miniature selves
Caught smiling on the mantlepiece,
Delighted it could be so simple.

Elizabeth, Elizabeth, what can I tell you –
How the comforting life of car explorations,
Or the polaroid guides to the narrative

Ignores the constant filling of the waterbarrels
And the nocturnal gauze of happenings
As natural events for sleeping through?

PRAYING MANTIS

The praying mantis
is resigned to death.

Bleak stones in his eyes
are locked staring
from his brine yellow skin.

A watching in-
sect drowsing on
the scrambler floor,

his hands are bent
in homage, body geometry
tensed and subdued.

Like a pilgrim
his love making
crowds death

into a religion
with the calm and the isolate
as his safety.

He breeds on the blind
and the illogic of rarity.
Killer within the law.

I am an outlaw
if I kill him.

2. Unregistered Papers

CHEMOTHERAPY

Tensing on the trip-switch of mustard gas
A pillow smell can now set off distress.
The nurse rounding my corridor of glass
Holds her neat tray, her lipped capsule's largesse.

SAILING INTO LEITRIM VILLAGE

William Glenn guides us to Leitrim Village –
Through the cuttings that furrow off the map,
Along the drains and bleak pumping stations
Where high water often floods
And a towpath battens down
Its parodic table of love seats.
In this calm wet New Barbary,
In the days that submerge the year,
We join the chatter of leavings, great events,
Where in an olive-stained drinking bar,
Through the dark of Ireland's holy hour,
We drift into the words of marriage.

From this end slip
We could circle in our own length,
Steer the blue margin of the marine file,
Nuzzling red and black
On British government charts of another century.
But the echo-sounder bleats,
The bell-stove smokes alarmingly,
And though the balm from the doldrums' stray fog
Unfurls in the rivers and lakes,
We search for the perfect hide.
These years letting the spirit subside
Have made us nonchalant with time.

A DIAMOND FOR HER THROAT

Your words today, admonish, instruct, and coil
      down the page
Like the seamless undulations I once showed you
Of an exhausted marsh near the sea.

Might the tide here so long gone, wait somewhere
      out of view,
To raise our marriage bed and trail us through
That diminishing air, that congruence
      of unlikely events?

I rake the mulching leaves, assorted browns of
      bark and carrion,
And while October fog descends, this quiet
      mild surround
Anticipates frost, a wrinkling quilt waiting to be tossed.

ST. CHARLES WARD

The nightwalkers drag contagion
Down the long corridors.
Staring at Dublin's mailboat
They imagine the flags of the Titanic,
Or its ghostly flotilla,
Gliding out to formulize
The wreck of the Greenwich meridian.
However confident the world works,
Days blur here,
Twilight fuses the bleached phosphorescence,
Taps mimic the unnamed waterfalls,
And in the corner of the room,
Near the curtained sluice alcove
Something bright evolves,
Our menu reader slurs his lines,
My old friend is helped down
To the transplant ward,
And one by one we sign off
With a nod and a smile.

MATT KIERNAN

He tries to explain
How a gift emerges
Singing from the shadows,

How holding the reamer like a baton
Conducts receding melodies,

And how rhythm runs
Like a finger through a stencil in his brain.

The radio light trembles,
And the battery bleeds in its cage,
So when at last he plays

The air is as true
As the quiet inflection of easter snow
Settling in its drifts of blue.

UNREGISTERED PAPERS

With mild interrogations I prompt
Computer tickings to retrieve marginalia –
Obscure replies for my buff file

From the dust offices in Newcastle and Chelsea.
As though verifying the past all day
Would carbon date love's minutiae

And all this could set geigers
To predict the fahrenheit failures,
Explain the meandering of the swaying sun,

Or trace the moon tug that lapses
Yet is endless and ascendant somewhere.
While the mosaic of tax lines assemble

My visitants flex copper-thin wrists,
And their arms splay, like the chalky sinews
Of London's navvy underground.

TRAVELLING LIGHT

Before Christmas, the small gatherings
In banks and corporate offices, afterhours,
Mime the end-of-year parties.

I watch a brave middle-income troupe
In St. Martin-in-the-Fields
Rehearse the *St. Matthew Passion*,

Unseasonal scores, a birth not a death,
And momentarily forgotten,
Their cars, their frail insignia,

Speed underground back
To the flotilla of wharfs and gardens,
Where threadbare estate lines

Haphazardly define that otherness
From me, and these drowsy London Irish tramps,
Who stretch and snore in the heated pews.

When, head in hand, your face emerges,
A young woman invoking the Messiah –
Blond neck bare, strings of beads

Rolled between the lynx light hairs –
I relax to imbibe that phrasing,
Performed time and time over

Like instinct or a commandment,
And know these sometimes lines are the ties
That will reluctantly, if eventually, define.

THE PLOVER'S SHORE

Built in the Eisenhower years
When the census mercury slowed to a tilt,
Our New England home

Settled on its grains of bevelled glass.
Relaxing in what passes for autumn here
We stray now, like hoboes on the edge of the Atlantic

Trying to find that cattleprod inlet
Where some Marian monks
Drill their cross with a tractor pitch

And imagine the whole wide horizon
Evoked in their spirals of praying.
In the search for a dervish calm

I saw white lint rise in the air
And the silence echoed in steely beds
Was the drone as names reveal the fields,

A hum detailed in the fontanells.
Our dreams lapse in a watery doze,
They hibernate on the lake floor,

And we might be the only pair left to tell
Of that ache in its silent repose,
The language of the plover's shore.

MILLER VIEWS LOS ALAMOS

The way our parishes deplete
Has allowed the saplings
To multiply in the dew.

These serene colonizations
Are logical strips of elm
Extending to my door,

And if there is no evil intention
Might some nerve
Shudder in the scent of power?

Or do we all try to arrange our lives
Watching one another
With mild surprise?

And if the sea should fall,
Could we reinvent the horizon
Or die after all?

In the swarm of tonight's radio
An awkward motif
Is *Midnight In Moscow*,

Yet ribbons of land
Now fulfil the imagination
Of Franklin's last stand.

And the parallax line
That falters in occasional fog
Was there all the time.

Coyotes have appeared in the wood.

SKETCHES FOR *FILM NOIR*

From the window of this hotel room
I see the uptown office
Sweltering as it turns away from light.

Deep in the margins of these afterhours,
In the dun conveyance of apartment houses,
Words like 'alimony' or 'realty',

Animate the couple
Who have just walked in from the street.
The fan has been dismantled for repair,

And though there is latent mischief,
This is not serious.
The man who gestures to a fault

Will explain the value of nothing,
And in the time it takes to inch the door ajar,
Someone teases out the frame.

IS THIS A SAFE PLACE, OR WHAT?

Even the greatness of Beechey's journeys
Dims illegibly by the light in this cabin.
In the drowsy odour of kerosene
Fuse elements expose,
And in the dewy interludes
Where we built our seamless lives,
Tears dissolve the day.
As the boat slaps on its beaded moorings,
Cars thread the inlet slips
And two by two, frail magenta lights
Echo music down the bones of old darkness,
Setting off minute timbre bells,
That let us doze in the slippage of dreams.

We are shelved in the lea of the lough's great loves,
Tied to the wooden levee –
And the hurricane lamp sauntering on the
          imaginary bank
Could be Wolfe or Beechey
Pencilling the boils on Adelaide Rock.
But is this a safe place, or what?
Do our grieving mistresses still entreat *The Times,*
Pretending one more lost soul
Is important in their lives?
Or are we always monitored somewhere,
Just failing to return from the lakes
For the start of another week.